You know you need to do this.

I know you can!

D. VINCENT WILLIAMS & PHILLIP WHITE

INTRODUCTION BY RASCAL FLATTS

I'm Movin' On

finding peace with yourself

RUTLEDGE HILL PRESS™

Nashville, Tennessee

A DIVISION OF THOMAS NELSON, INC.

www.ThomasNelson.com

Published by Rutledge Hill Press, a division of Thomas Nelson, Inc., P.O. Box 141000,
Nashville, Tennessee 37214

Design: Karen Phillips

ISBN: 1-4016-0006-9

Printed in the United States of America

02 03 04 05 06 — 5 4 3 2 1

THANKS

To my wonderful wife, Amber, for always being there • Jordyn and Jackson for being great kids (I'm so proud of you both) • my mom and dad for being my rock • Glen, Janet, and April (Gram, Papa, and Auntie) for being the shoulder my family leans on • My brothers (Faron, Darryl, and Eric) for all the crazy times we've had and the memories that still make me smile • David Vincent Williams for sharing this wonderful time with me • Jimmy Melton for your knowledge of the Roland • Paul Compton for getting "I'm Movin' On" cut • Mark Bright for hearing it • Mark, Marty Williams, and Rascal Flatts (Gary, Jay, and Joe Don) for cutting such a great record • Lyric Street Records for putting the single out • radio for playing the song • Roger Murrah for giving me the opportunity to write songs for a living • my family at Murrah Music (Lissa, Dan, Rachel, Jimmy, Neal, Luke, Roger F., Ray, Joe, Spence, Bart, Leigh) for getting me through the past five years • J. Aaron Brown for my first job • Spooner Oldham for getting me started • Kris Kristoferson and Paul Overstreet for being great heroes • Everyone who has been a part of my life and who has given me something to write about • Berkley and Castaway for helping me reach new goals every day • Rutledge Hill Press for allowing us to write this book • Bryan Curtis for your honest opinion • And most of all, GOD for all the incredible blessings in my life.

—PHILLIP WHITE

I wish I could do the impossible and thank every person that played a part in "I'm Movin' On"! That goes for the song, as well as the book. It has been an experience that I will treasure for a lifetime.

With that said, the writing of this book may have been the most rewarding part of the whole thing. It gave Phillip and me a chance to reflect on the writing appointment and all the years of chance and change, the inspiring elements, meat and potatoes you might say, that were the creating factors of the song and the book.

First I would like to thank 1997. If it hadn't been for that year and all the trials that came along with it, I would never have had the insight or the courage to attempt such a feat. I would also like to thank you, Phillip, for your patience, support, and talents. Meeting you by chance is one of the best things that has ever happened to me, and I will always consider you to be one of my best friends. To my wife, I would like to say thanks for hanging in there with me and giving me two wonderful children. Now we can see that our experience did have a purpose. You're the greatest! Thanks to Richard Orga and Tim Wipperman for all of your support, even through the LEAN years. And thanks to Bryan Curtis and Larry Stone at Rutledge Hill Press for giving two old country boys a shot at being authors (that still sounds weird!).

A special thanks to Rascal Flatts and their team for their talents and delivery of our song. You guys have given us a much needed breath of fresh air.

I want to truly thank Devon O' Day, Gerry House, and Paul Compton! If it weren't for you guys, "I'm Movin' On" would never have seen the light of day. As for Devon and Gerry, you are an example of the power of radio and its listeners. Without you both, I wouldn't even be writing this thank you letter. By the way, we still have a steak dinner to go to, obviously OUR TREAT!

To all I am forgetting, I'm sorry . . . and grateful for your contribution to the success of "I'm Movin' On"! Thanks again, and God bless.

—D. VINCENT WILLIAMS

I'm Movin' On

D. Vincent Williams/Phillip White

I've dealt with my ghosts and I've faced all my demons

Finally content with a past I regret

I've found you find strength in your moments of weakness

For once I'm at peace with myself

I've been burdened with blame, trapped in the past for too long...

I'm movin' on

I've lived in this place and I know all the faces

Each one is different but they're always the same

They mean me no harm but it's time that I face it

They'll never allow me to change

But I never dreamed home would end up where I don't belong...

I'm movin' on

Chorus:

I'm movin' on,

At last I can see life has been patiently waiting for me

And I know there's no guarantees, but I'm not alone

There comes a time in everyone's life

When all you can see are the years passing by

And I have made up my mind that those days are gone

I sold what I could and packed what I couldn't

Stopped to fill up on my way out of town

I've loved like I should but I lived like I shouldn't

I had to lose everything to find out

Maybe forgiveness will find me somewhere down this road...

I'm movin' on

    I'm movin' on

        I'm movin' on

We were in the studio recording our debut album when we sat down with our producers one morning to listen to more songs. We must have went through three thousand tunes on this day, the day we discovered "I'm Movin' On." We were acquainted with the songwriters, Phillip White and D. Vincent Williams, and became aware that this tune was the evolution and confession of a very personal experience for one of them. It was an honor to be given the opportunity to bring to life this story in a song. An artist can wait a lifetime or career to find a gem like this. We were humbled to be a part of their masterpiece.

RASCAL FLATTS

Gary Levox

Jay DeMarcus

Joe Don Rooney

Forewords

It was three o'clock in the morning and I just couldn't sleep. In three short years I had successfully lost my wife, my daughter, my recording contract; damaged my relationship with my father, sister, and mother; and put myself in over $90,000 of debt. But this night would change my life, forever. For the first time something told me that maybe, just maybe, it wasn't everybody else's fault. With tears in my eyes, I asked, "Why is this happening to me?" I was at the bottom! All I wanted to do was run away. I rolled over to the piano next to my bed, in the dark, and played the introduction melody to "I'm Movin' On." Seeing that it was four in the morning and that I had a writing appointment the next day with Phillip White, someone I had never met before, I thought I should get some sleep. Little did I know that the Creator himself had just put the wheels of serenity in motion.

The next morning I woke up with that melody ringing in my ears and wondering how I was going to convince my cowriter that I was the happiest person on earth. Needless to say, I failed! He looked at me and said "Man, are you OK?" For a moment I thought about asking him if we could reschedule for another day, but something very interesting happened—I just started telling him everything. I was amazed at his compassion and concern and, though I couldn't see it, I had just made one of the best friends of my life!

He said, "Let's just write about it." So I played him the melody I had stumbled on the night before and he looked at me and said, "I got it!" His next words were "I've dealt with my ghosts and I've faced all my demons." It was something he had written years before and he had been waiting for the right time to bring it to light. That single-handedly started the most healing experience of my life. We shared the different kinds of scars and wounds we had acquired over the years as well as the triumphs and successes. We laughed, we cried, and we watched as "I'm Movin' On" became a reality!

—D. Vincent Williams

I will never forget the day D. Vincent Williams walked into my office. I looked at him and said, "How are you doing?" He said, "My wife left, I haven't seen my daughter in months, and I'm just trying my best to get through each day." As David spilled his guts to me, I realized I had unfinished business of my own.

I needed to spend more time with my kids. I needed to call my mom and dad and say "I love you." I needed to tell my wife I couldn't live without her.

"I'm Movin' On" has changed my life forever. Not only has it given me a whole new outlook on dealing with my problems, but it's also brought me peace with things I've been dealing with for years. I still have my share of demons to deal with, but I can't help feeling that with each breath I'm given comes a new chance. . . . a new beginning. This song has been a huge blessing to me and I hope this book will be to you.

—Phillip White

Moving On

The Inevitable Reality

You're in trouble! Lately, your life just isn't making much sense. Somewhere along the way you lost touch with all those dreams and plans you made years ago. You find yourself staring at this person in the mirror you don't even recognize. You have trouble believing you actually settled for that dead-end job you swore you wouldn't do. Of course you can't just quit! Somehow you let your finances get completely out of control, which has put a heavy burden on the relationship between you and your significant other. It feels like your life is spiraling down an endless mountain of regret.

But wait a minute...you come from a good family and you are a fairly decent person, so you should know what to do, how to handle it, right?...WRONG! You seem to be losing every good thing in your life in what seems like a matter of moments. Your first impulse is to run, but what good would that do? If your situation is anything like mine was, you're probably starting to get the feeling that the man upstairs is trying to tell you something!

This book is not intended to preach, judge, or criticize. Nor does it claim to hold the answers to all of life's problems. It is solely a collection of truths, thoughts, and similar experiences shared by two good friends, all brought to light when the song "I'm Movin' On" came to life. Although our paths were different, our stories were the same.

We all reach "moving on" points in our lives and this book is a little reminder that whoever you are, wherever you live, no matter where you come from or wherever you're going... somebody's been there before!

The only true constant is... change!

So why fight it?

Our lives are continually changing. They have been changing since we were born. And with change comes the result of change... Moving On!

If you relate so far and if you're still reading... you have already made the first step!

Awareness

There comes a time in everyone's life

✳

I remember waking up late one night craving a big glass of cold water. I had to maneuver my way around in the dark until I made it to the living room. After successfully dodging the recliner and the coffee table, I realized that I needed to sit down to give my eyes some time to adjust. After a few minutes I could make out the silhouettes of my surroundings and I got up off the couch and hurried to the kitchen for that glass of water. I made it about halfway through the dining room when I stubbed my toe on a toy my son had forgotten to pick up. While experiencing what I considered to be excruciating pain, I immediately began cussing the toy while making plans to reprimand my son for leaving it there.

The moral of this true story is ...

you may be able to adapt to the DARK,

your eyes can adjust to the DARK,

but you're still in the **DARK!**

For a good part of my life I stumbled around in

darkness, thinking I could see well enough to get

where I needed to go before I became AWARE of the

problem. And needless to say, I stubbed my toe

several times on life's little building blocks.

But the fact remains ...

I would have never hurt myself

if I had just ...

turned the light on!

IN THE DARK:

What you can't see can hurt you.

WITH A LITTLE LIGHT:

What you couldn't see sticks out

like a sore thumb!

Or should I say...

Sore toe!

Acknowledgment

I've loved
like I
should but
lived like
I shouldn't.

Let's face it! Realizing that you have some problems isn't that difficult. It's usually obvious. To acknowledge **WHY** they exist is the hard part and is often very demoralizing. When you start to realize that the person you thought you were doesn't come close to being the person other people see in you, it comes as quite a shock. Sometimes it takes the hours turning into days and the days into weeks and the weeks into months and the months into years before you realize that something went wrong along the way.

But **WHY** it happened is the big question. And the search for the answer is ultimately one person's responsibility... **YOURS.**

What good is a comforting smile,

A heart full of love,

And endless acts of good intention,

When your life doesn't back it up?

In my first couple years of adulthood I ran around living in a fantasy world. I spent money I didn't have, thinking it would magically appear in my bank account. I had big dreams with no idea of how to reach them. I had been in a relationship two years longer than I should have and was convinced it was going to work out.

Everyone was my friend and I was a friend to everyone... or so it seemed. But one night I realized I wasn't meeting my full potential. I was going nowhere fast and there was only one person that could change that outcome ... ME!

So for the first time I asked myself the questions that for years I had ignored.

ASK YOURSELF...

Are my dreams coming true?

Am I where I want to be?

Are my friends really my friends?

Am I being realistic?

Do I like who I am?

Do I need to take more chances?

Do I need to change?

HOW DO I CHANGE?

AUTHOR'S NOTE—

Did you think we weren't going to get you involved?
Grab some paper—open your heart—and help yourself.

And after I acknowledged each of my questions,

I found the answers to them all!

ONE DAY AT A TIME...

HONESTLY!

They'll never allow me to change

It takes a long time to get honest with yourself. I was convinced I was happy even though I seldom felt joy. I was convinced I was strong even when I was at my weakest. I was convinced that my problems were mere setbacks and didn't amount to anything too serious. I was convinced I was in control.

The truth... I was not happy, not strong, overwhelmed, and completely out of control! Honest has been, by far, the most difficult thing for me to be with myself. I continually find that I am not as honest as I should be. Simply put... it makes us vunerable!

How do you tell a friend that his actions don't show true friendship? How do you tell someone you have invested years with that it's not going to work out? How do you accept that you, yourself, are unreliable, inconsiderate, lazy, or irresponsible? Yet we all suffer from these traits at some time in our lives.

The truth is... when we get honest, we stand to lose some of our comfort zone. Good or bad, when we know what's coming, we feel safer. Even when it's a freight train!

As a kid, I was a huge baseball fan. I remember watching some of my boyhood idols announcing their retirement. For years I never understood why these big men would cry on television, in front of the entire country. After all, these guys made millions doing what they loved—playing a kid game and making people happy every time they hit a home run, made a diving catch, or slid into home plate.

That's when it hit me...Hank Aaron and Mark McGwire can only hit so many home runs. Nolan Ryan can only strike out so many people. Ozzie Smith can only turn so many double plays.

At some point their fast ball isn't as fast as it used to be, and their bat can't get around quick enough to hit that new young gun. Sure, behind those tears is a true love of the game, but I can't imagine, after having been on top of their profession for years, having to stand in front of millions and say, "I just don't have it anymore." Wow!

Still, I can't help wondering:

Which was harder?

Having to admit it to millions

or

Having to admit it to themselves

Honesty...

The difference between

LIVING

and LIVING A LIE

Inventory

I've dealt with
my ghosts and
I've faced all
my demons, . . .
I've found you
find strength
in your moments
of weakness

After realizing that strength comes from admitting weakness, you can take a good look at your shortcomings without feeling the need to beat yourself up. Before I truly accepted that I was not perfect, I had a difficult time acknowledging my shortcomings. I had to get honest with myself. Once I did that, it was inventory time. I had to make the next move and take the time to make a list of the good, bad, and indifferent in my life. Guilt, unfortunately, is one of the by-products, but once you inventory your life, I bet you will feel a lot better and—believe it or not—a lot stronger.

AT LEAST I DID!

"Ghosts"

Those haunting little creatures that find

pleasure in frightening us, keeping us up

long exhausting hours in the night,

sneaking up behind us, and

jarring our guts, as if to say,

"And you thought you got rid of me!"

Ghosts? Or Guilt?

One summer I worked part-time for a swimming pool company. When I walked into their fifty-thousand-square-foot warehouse, I noticed, neatly organized, old pools with missing parts, worn out filter systems, and some stuff I couldn't have told you its purpose if you asked me to. I wondered why this company would spend money on such a big warehouse just to house a bunch of useless junk. So I asked my manager why in the world they did it. He just smiled and said, "We make $100,000 a year selling these not-so-easy-to-find parts to pool companies all over the world."

You see, everything—even your mistakes—has a purpose. Like that swimming pool company, you should store those hard-learned lessons in the back of your mind. When you find yourself at life's next crossroad, you'll have a warehouse full of priceless experience to steer you in the right direction.

Action

I've been burdened with blame, trapped in the past for too long...

I'm movin' on

I had a cousin (single, lonely, and absolutely beautiful) in her twenties. Every time I would see her, I would ask, "Have you found a boyfriend?" She always answered, "No, but I'm praying about it." Then I'd say, "Do you ever go to the singles class at church or anything?" She always answered, "No, but I'm praying about it." Finally I asked her, "Has anyone asked you out?" She answered, "Several times, but I feel I need to pray about it first."

You can pray until you're blue in the face and throw a million dollars worth of pennies in a wishing well, but until you put feet beneath your prayers and legs under your dreams and meet God halfway, you're going to have a difficult time finding what you're looking for!

This is it!

This morning, get up and

swallow your pride,

hold your chin high,

and let your guard down.

Stop kicking yourself about things

that happened yesterday.

Today is a new day, a fresh start,

and a clean slate.

Make the most of it!

Believe in fate!

Just don't rely on it.

Move On

Move On!

> Maybe forgiveness will find me somewhere down this road

When you're in the sixth grade, you can't wait to get to high school. When you're in high school, you can't wait to go to college. When you're in college, you can't wait to go to work. When you're working, you can't wait to retire. But when you retire, you look back at all the precious moments you wasted wishing you were somewhere else.

What's the rush? You're going to get there.

So sit back and enjoy the ride.

You see, we often want

immediate results. But we all know that's

very unrealistic. It took most of us years to get in the

situation we find ourselves. And it's going to take as long to

get where we want—or need—to go. Patience is not an easy gift

to give yourself. It goes against what we see— fast food restaurants,

one-hour film developing, thirty-second commercials with at least

five minutes worth of gibberish. We need not confuse convenience

with quality. In order to have a satisfying life, we need to appreciate

the value of patience.

Tomorrow is...

Tomorrow is...a new beginning

Tomorrow is...one more chance

Tomorrow is...H O P E

Tomorrow is...going to be better

Tomorrow is...what you make it

Tomorrow is...just a few hours away

Tomorrow is...the first day of the rest of your life

Tomorrow is...WORTH WAITING FOR!

ASK YOURSELF...

What is one thing I can do today that will make my
life better immediately?

What is one thing I hope/dream about
happening when I make this change?
(And I will make this change!)

Why am I afraid?

Who loves me?

Who will be there for me—no matter what?

Your life is going to get better.

Acceptance

Finally
content
with a past
I regret

About seven years ago, I met a twenty-one-year-old girl with a four-year-old daughter. You do the math! She became pregnant when she was seventeen. I asked her how she dealt with that, and she told me she was depressed during her entire pregnancy. She felt she had lost her childhood. She never thought she would find someone to love her with a kid on her hip. She also told me that the minute she held that baby in her arms everything else disappeared. She accepted the fact that she was a teenage parent. She accepted the fact that she was still young even though she was a mother. She also accepted the fact that she would one day find someone to love her more than anything else on this earth.

GOD, I'M GLAD SHE DID!

You see, if she hadn't,

I wouldn't have my

beautiful step-daughter,

my son, my wife... MY LIFE!

—PHILLIP WHITE

It's time that I accept
The bad as well as good
The blessings in my failures
The way I know I should

It's time that I accept
The lows as well as highs
Replace things I've done wrong
With things that I've done right

It's time that I accept
Bad choices that I've made
Against my better judgment
And give myself a break

It's time that I accept
These things I can't control
I know I've done my best
It's time that I accept!

The bad days don't come around

as often as they used to, and the

good ones tend to be more genuine.

You find yourself looking back and smiling

rather than reprimanding yourself.

It's kind of like bills that are due.

Once you put them down on paper

and make a planned attack, they

don't seem as impossible as they used to.

You start feeling better . . . inside and out!

Confession

I had
to lose
everything
to find out

Nothing is more difficult than having to recognize and own up to your failures. Believe me, I know. It took me thirty years to be completely honest with myself. It almost kills you to accept the fact that you took part in everything wrong in your life. But as you take the first steps, there is nothing like having a guiltless conscience to help steer you in the right direction.

It's hard to admit you are wrong.

But it sure feels good when you do.

Even if no one else knows... you do.

Even if no one else hears your confession... you do.

Even if no one else forgives you... you can!

YOU CAN'T UN-BURN A BRIDGE...

BUT YOU CAN BUILD A NEW ONE!

My Confession...

I was trying to please everyone. I wanted to prove to everyone around me that I was going to make it. The things I did for people were not for them, but for myself. I brought my mom, dad, and sister to Nashville not for their support, but so that they could watch me succeed. I blamed them when things didn't work out and watched them take on the guilt of my poor judgment. I spent three years convincing myself—and anyone who would listen—that the music industry was unfair. There is no telling how many young dreamers I crippled before they ever got a chance to walk!

I found out that it was all because I wanted to matter! I had to lose it all before I stopped the madness.

And guess what? As soon as I picked up the pieces and took some responsibility for my selfishness...

I made it!

How ironic!

—D. VINCENT WILLIAMS

ASK YOURSELF...

What have I failed at?

(that was way too easy)

What is something I really messed up?

What part did I play in it?

How can I correct my
mistake/failure/colossal
lapse of judgment?

How will my life get better if I can own up...
make it right...and move on?

own up / make it right / move on...

Amends

I've lived
in this place
and I know
all the faces
Each one
is different
but they're
always
the same
They mean
me no harm...

✕

No one is out to hurt you.

It took me a long time to actually believe that. In the process of figuring it out, I hurt a lot of people. Friends, family, and strangers all caught the brunt of my disappointments. We often choose blame over responsibility. We tell ourselves things like:

"Well if he hadn't"

"If only she would have just..."

"If someone would have just told me that..."

It's amazing how fast we pass judgment. If you were to list all the people who you felt were responsible for all the bad in your life, I bet your list would reach the floor. But what about the list of people you hurt, or judged, or blamed? I think that list would be somewhat shorter... don't you? As you begin to see the light, you also begin to realize the extent of the damage you caused by living in denial. Your blame list gets shorter while your victim list starts growing like a stinkweed! Give the people you hurt, judged, or blamed a call or write them a letter and just say "I'm sorry."

NO ONE CAN FORGIVE WITHOUT THE OPPORTUNITY!

AMEND

(1. to put right. 2. to change or modify for the better.)

We would do anything to salvage a relationship that means something to us. We would readily **CHANGE** to make our significant other happy. There's nothing wrong with **CHANGE** when it's for the better, but while you're thinking about ways to meet that certain someone's approval, think about the last time you changed something in your life for yourself. Think about it...

Every year on December 31, we tell ourselves, "I'm going to quit smoking," or "I'm going to stop drinking." How often do we follow through? So what's the point? Now think about this for a moment... How great would your life be if you kept every promise you made to yourself?

We put significant pressure on ourselves to keep our word when we're dealing with others. We don't like someone else to lie to us. So **WHY** do we lie to ourselves time after time after time?

Making amends is important in keeping our relationships with others strong and healthy. Do yourself a favor—when you make a promise to yourself, keep it! Your relationship with yourself will be stronger and healthier.

My Wish List

I wish I could take back every wrong word I ever said.

I wish I could undo everything I didn't do right.

I wish I could mend every heart that I've ever broken.

I wish I could dry every tear that I put in someone else's eye.

I wish I could

    I wish I could

        but I can't! But I can say... I'm sorry.

ASK YOURSELF...

Who am I holding a grudge against?

What could I do with that time and energy
I spend holding a grudge?

Who should I forgive—even
if they haven't asked? Think of
the burden that will be lifted
from your heart.

Who do I need to apologize to?

What do I need? What do I want to let go of?

How will this make my life better?

What are you doing sitting there?

Forgiveness

For once
I'm at
peace with
myself

※ To my dad for not showing up to my little league games, as well as me for wrecking his Buick LeSabre.

※ To my mom for giving me that one undeserved spanking, and me for the other hundreds I did deserve.

※ To my brother for serving me underage, and me for the stain I left on his carpet.

※ To my sister for causing so many family worries, and me for not having enough faith in her.

※ To Kristi for breaking my heart, and me for breaking Sally's heart.

※ To Derrick, my friend, for dying too young, and me for not saying "I love you."

※ To my son for messing up his room, and me for losing my temper.

※ To my daughter for jumping on the couch, and me for not realizing that it was a plea for some well-deserved attention.

※ To my wife for having second thoughts, and me for putting them there.

※ To God...the only one who never let me down, and me for the years that I blamed him.

I'm extending and asking for . . . *Forgiveness!*

Sweet forgiveness!

That little reminder that

you're not perfect... and it's OK!

This is a big one. Maybe the biggest of them all.

There are two types of forgiveness:

offering and accepting

First and foremost, forgive yourself. You have to forgive yourself before you are truly capable of asking for or extending forgiveness to anyone or anything else.

Second, forgive the victims. We all have our prisoners. Once and for all, ask for forgiveness and set them free!

Third, forgive your enemies. This is a toughie! It's easier to ask for forgiveness from your victims than it is to offer it to your enemies. Just remember, some of your victims view you as one of their enemies. If you can't offer... they won't accept!

And don't forget your maker. If it wasn't for the forgiveness of our maker, none of us would stand a chance. While he's still offering forgiveness... do yourself a favor and take it.

Amazing grace!

How sweet the sound

that saved a wretch like me!

I once was lost

but now am found,

was blind but now I see.

I sold what
I could and
packed what
I couldn't

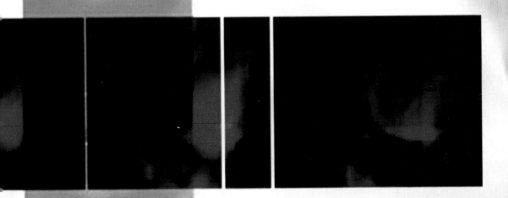

It's time to strike that imaginary match and burn all the regrets, bad choices, wrong turns, and the rest of that junk that's been keeping you from getting where you need to be. I don't know what it is about humans and their junk, but it is definitely time for a garage sale! I promise... you won't miss it.

I never did!

Sold some

Gave some away

Threw some out

BUT I KEPT

THE GOOD STUFF...

GOOD RIDDANCE!...

Things I shouldn't have let go of:	Things I need to let go of:	Things I'm glad I let go of:
My first guitar	Regrets	Whiskey sours
My first car	Credit cards	One of my car payments
My granddaddy's shotgun	Chocolate	Low self-esteem
Those unfinished songs	Half the clothes in my closet	That hot pot with the metal handle . . . where did I get that thing, anyway?
My brother's rod and reel when that big bass surprised me		

There was a time in my life when being miserable was the norm for me. You wouldn't have recognized me with a smile on my face. Bitterness was a part of my life and complaining was a part of my daily routine. I was comfortable being the grouch I had become. Thank heaven above, I woke up and saw the light and traded that security blanket of misery for a quilt of contentment!

MovingOn

At last
I can see
life has
been patiently
waiting for me

Fear! This is the leading cause of unfulfilled dreams and aspirations. Yet we can never quite put our finger on what it is that we are so afraid of. And we usually look back and realize that there was nothing to be afraid of in the first place. Don't allow yourself to sit idle and watch the world leave you behind. If you need to quit that job, leave that town, rekindle that relationship, or anything else your gut might be begging you to do, for your sake...do it!

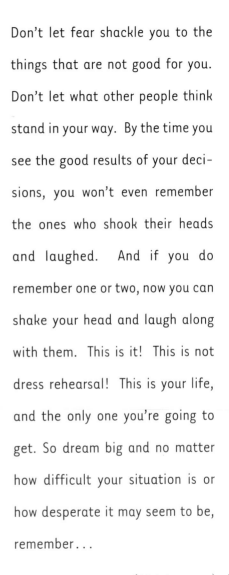

Don't let fear shackle you to the things that are not good for you. Don't let what other people think stand in your way. By the time you see the good results of your decisions, you won't even remember the ones who shook their heads and laughed. And if you do remember one or two, now you can shake your head and laugh along with them. This is it! This is not dress rehearsal! This is your life, and the only one you're going to get. So dream big and no matter how difficult your situation is or how desperate it may seem to be, remember...

(this is important) →

You are not alone!

You have never

been alone!

And you'll
never be alone!

Your emotional bags are packed...

Move On!

Move On!

Move On!

YOU'RE READY!